The Day Miss Grouchy Melted

A Low-Stress Christmas Program

Mel Ann Coley

CSS Publishing Company, Inc., Lima, Ohio

I0214157

THE DAY MISS GROUCHY MELTED

Copyright © 2000 by
CSS Publishing Company, Inc.
Lima, Ohio

All rights reserved. No part of this publication may be reproduced in any manner whatsoever without the prior permission of the publisher, except in the case of brief quotations embodied in critical articles and reviews. Inquiries should be addressed to: Permissions, CSS Publishing Company, Inc., P.O. Box 4503, Lima, Ohio 45802-4503.

For more information about CSS Publishing Company resources, visit our website at www.csspub.com.

ISBN 0-7880-1763-2   PRINTED IN U.S.A.

Dedicated to
my sweet family
who have transformed me
with their kindness

Author's Notes

This play provides a way for your church to produce a *low-stress* Christmas program! How? First of all, trying to memorize lines for a play is stressful for most children. In this play the narrator tells the story, and the children simply "act out" certain parts that are marked in the script. Secondly, any number of characters can easily be added or deleted to play the roles of the students. Last of all, this format allows for many ages to participate. Typically, an older child will play the character of Miss Grouchy. Middle-aged children can play the parts of Rachel and David. The younger children can act out giving Miss Grouchy gifts.

With all of these factors, this play can be rehearsed a few times and easily produced. At the first rehearsal, read the entire story and select the characters. Then walk through the story and discuss how to act out the various situations. Ask the characters to bring the few props that are needed from home to the next rehearsal. All in all, this play promises a uniquely different program!

Characters:

Narrator

Miss Grouchy

Rachel

David

Rachel's Mom

David's Mom

Other Students (any number)

The Day Miss Grouchy Melted

(The narrator begins reading the story as Miss Grouchy enters with her coat on)

Even though the sun was shining brightly and it was a beautiful day, Miss G still wore her heavy, brown coat to teach her class at Fields Elementary School. She always wore her coat — no matter what kind of weather it was! Some of the older students whispered that it was because she had such a cold heart that she couldn't stay warm without her coat.

(The narrator continues to read the story, and the students act like they are talking behind her back)

Although no one knew if this was true, they did know she never smiled. She never said, "Good work." She never said, "Please." And they knew her name was so hard to pronounce that she had finally just shortened it to "Miss G." But behind her back the students said the "G" stood for grouchy, so they secretly called her Miss Grouchy.

(Miss Grouchy pretends to pace around the students as the narrator reads the story)

The days seemed to last forever in Miss G's class. Miss G didn't allow any smiling or laughing. "Work, work, work," she would say as she paced around the classroom tapping her ruler on the students' desks.

(Rachel acts as if she is talking to her mom, and the narrator continues to read)

Finally, a smart student named Rachel came up with a plan she hoped would end Miss G's grouchiness. It all started because Rachel's mom was a volunteer at Fields Elementary School; she helped with any special events that the school planned. One day Rachel's mom told her, "It's so close to Christmas, why don't you and the other children surprise Miss G with gifts?"

At first Rachel didn't want to do anything for such a grouchy person. But then her mom said, "I love parties; they just make me smile all day."

"I love Christmas parties too — especially the presents," Rachel thought. Then she got an idea! "I wonder if giving Miss G presents would make her be happy too?" she wondered. She decided it was surely worth trying.

(Rachel pretends to tell all of the other students at recess, and they act out their agreement to her plan. Then they exit the stage)

The next day at recess Rachel told everyone about the plan to surprise Miss G with gifts at a Christmas party. All of the students agreed that if gifts could cheer up their grouchy teacher, they would do it.

(The narrator continues to read while David and his mom act out a conversation)

But that night when one of the students named David asked his mom for money to buy a gift, she shook her head. Then she said, "I don't have any money left from my paycheck. But you have some drawing paper and crayons, so why don't you make her a nice card?"

(The narrator reads and David acts as if he is drawing a card)

David was disappointed about the gift, but he didn't want to be the only one without something to give Miss G. So he made a beautiful card with flowers, sunshine, and birds on it. But when he opened it up to write something nice in it, he couldn't think of what to say to such a grouchy person. And he knew it was wrong to lie.

(Next, David asks his mom and she pretends to whisper)

6

Finally, he asked his mom, and she smiled. Then she bent down and whispered in his ear. Then he smiled, too, and ran to his room to finish the card.

(David and his mom exit the stage; he rejoins the rest of the students. Students then act out yelling and running up to the desk)

On Friday, all the students yelled, "Surprise!" as Miss G walked in the door. Then they all ran up to her desk with what they had brought.

(As the narrator continues to read, Miss Grouchy acts out her part, and the children pretend to give her gifts)

But Miss G did not look happy about her Christmas surprise. She put her hands on her hips, looked down her long nose and over her small, black glasses as she said, "No running. No yelling. Line up if you expect me to open these gifts."

As she opened each beautifully-wrapped gift, she simply mumbled a very quiet "Thank you." Then she said in her grouchy voice, "Next!"

(David pretends to be afraid as the narrator continues)

Finally it was David's turn, and he wanted to crawl under her big desk and hide. But Miss G had already seen his card. So she asked in her deep voice, "And what do you have, David?"

Since David had always been a little bit afraid of Miss G, his hand was shaking as he handed her the card. Miss G looked at the card with the flowers, sunshine, and birds on it, but she still did not smile. Then she opened it up and read aloud to the class what was written inside.

(Miss Grouchy acts out reading the card)

She read, "Thank you for teaching me so many things."

(Miss G pretends to faint and wake up smiling as the narrator continues)

Then a strange thing happened. Miss G fainted and hit the floor with a loud thud! But before any of the students could go for help, she woke up. Then she sat up and smiled!

(Miss G acts as if she is taking off her coat, pulling her hair, and fanning herself as the narrator continues)

"Oh, my goodness, it's so hot in here," Miss G said as she took off her coat! They she pulled her hair up into a ponytail, and fanned herself with her hand.

(The students stare while Miss G thanks them)

All of the students were staring at Miss G because she didn't look the same way without her coat. And she certainly didn't act the same way either when she smiled and said, "Thank you all so much for the gifts."

(While the narrator reads, David and Miss G pretend to talk. Then Miss G pats her heart)

The students were all still wondering what had happened when Miss G leaned down to talk to David. In a soft voice she said, "Your gift was very special to me." And as she said this, she placed her hand over her heart, gave it a soft pat, and sighed. Then they all knew what had happened.

(At this point, darken the lights and have everyone except the narrator exit. Then spotlight the narrator as the final paragraph is read)

The students knew that the warmth from David's kind words had melted Miss G's ice-cold heart! So from this day on, Miss G never came to Fields Elementary School with her heavy, brown coat on unless it was really cold outside. She always smiled as she said, "Please," and "Good work." And no one ever called her Miss Grouchy again.

8

www.ingramcontent.com/pod-product-compliance
Lightning Source LLC
Chambersburg PA
CBHW070044040426
42331CB00033B/2502

9780788017636